Love in a Fearful Land
A Guatemalan Story

Other books by Henri J.M. Nouwen
published by Ave Maria Press

With Open Hands

Out of Solitude

In Memoriam

Love in a Fearful Land
A Guatemalan Story

Henri J. M. Nouwen

Photography by Peter K. Weiskel

AVE MARIA PRESS
NOTRE DAME, IN 46556

Acknowledgments:

Scripture quotations in this book are taken from *The Jerusalem Bible,* copyright ©
1966 by Darton Longman & Todd, Ltd. and Doubleday & Company, Inc. Used
with permission of the publisher.

Excerpts from the Information Bulletin of the Guatemala Human Rights Commis-
sion/U.S.A. and from the Bimonthly Publications of Latin America Documentation
(LADOC) are used with permission.

© 1985 by Ave Maria Press

Library of Congress Catalog Card Number: 85-71913

International Standard Book Number: 0-87793-294-8

Cover and text design: Thomas Ringenberg

Printed and bound in the United States of America.

*We dedicate this book
to the Indian people of Guatemala,
whose courage, perseverance and deep faith
have given us a new glimpse
of the dignity of the human heart
and offered us new hope for peace.*

Stan Rother blessing some of his parishioners. (Photo by Frankie Williams)

*A*cknowledgments

Although this is a small book written in a short time, many people spent much time in bringing it from a first draft to a publishable text. I want to express my deep gratitude to Phil Zaeder and Richard Alan White for their many constructive comments concerning both the form and content of the manuscript. Peter Weiskel spent many days integrating their suggestions into the final text and made many contributions of his own in the final stage of editing. Without his patient assistance this book would never have been finished.

A special word of thanks goes to Mrs. Frankie Williams, Father David Monahan and Sister Marita Rother for their help in verifying the many facts to which we allude throughout the book. I also owe a debt of true gratitude to Kay Shanahan for her generous and dedicated secretarial assistance.

The photography in this book is, with a few exceptions, the work of Peter Weiskel. Seldom have I been so glad to have a good friend accompany me on a journey who also happened to be a gifted photographer. Such was the situation with Peter, which helped lead to this book. The photographs on pages 8, 40, 51 and 66 were taken by Mrs. Frankie Williams. Photos from the Religious News Service and the *National Catholic Reporter* appear on pages 39 and 80 respectively.

The letters of Father Stanley Rother cited in this text were written during the last year of his life, and are referred to by date. An edition of these letters, entitled *The Shepherd Cannot Run*, was published by the Archdiocese of Oklahoma City in 1984.

Finally, I would like to thank Frank Cunningham, editor of Ave Maria Press, and those whom he asked to read the text, when we doubted the wisdom of publishing it. Their support and encouragement helped us greatly in overcoming our hesitations.

Stories to Be Told

This is the story of two men, both North Americans, both parish priests in Guatemala. Their names are Stanley Francis Rother and John Vesey. Stanley was murdered in Santiago Atitlán on July 28, 1981; three years later John went to Santiago Atitlán to take his place. This is also a story about the mysterious presence of a faithful God in the midst of a country ravaged by violence, torture and assassination. Most of all, it is a story about prayer. In the end, prayer summarizes the most needed response to the reality we encountered.

Rev. Stanley Francis Rother

Soon after John Vesey had received the news that Archbishop Charles Salatka of Oklahoma City had appointed him to the parish of Santiago Atitlán, he called me and said, "I want you to visit me and simply pray with me and the Indian people. . . . I am going there to pray and I want you to come too." I immediately sensed the importance of John's invitation. I had always felt that my friendship with John was a special gift of God, that without that friendship I never would have grasped the deeper meaning of my growing interest in the life of the church in Central and South America. Now that John's hope of taking Stanley Rother's place was finally being fulfilled, I knew that something new was beginning for me. His invitation was a call to take a new step, not only in our friendship but also down the longer road of our ongoing search for conversion.

One month after John had arrived at his new parish, I decided to accept his invitation. Rather than go alone, I asked my friend and co-worker Peter Weiskel to come with me. I knew that making this journey with Peter would prove fruitful, and that his talent for photography would allow us to tell the story in more than one way. I have often felt the need to write about my own painful and joyful experiences in the conviction that they were not meant to remain hidden. This time I anticipated that the story to be told would have a greater urgency than ever before, and that with Peter's help it could be a purer story, emerging from shared experiences, discoveries and visions.

Peter and I flew to Guatemala City on August 27, 1984, and arrived in Santiago Atitlán two days later. We returned to the United States on September 5th. During this ten-day journey we saw striking landscapes, met extraordinary people and participated in splendid ceremonies. But what finally made us tell this story is not so much the landscape, the people or the ceremonies, but the life of a martyr and the man who took his place. Stanley Rother's martyrdom needs to be told, for martyrs are blood witnesses of God's inexhaustible love for his people. Stan is such a martyr, and his story needs to be spread so that Christians everywhere will begin to think about Guatemala not just as a country darkened by violence, but primarily as a country which teaches us anew that "God sent his Son into the world not to condemn the world, but so that through him the world might be saved" (Jn 3:17).This story of martyrdom also concerns John Vesey, who took Stan's place to affirm through his presence the power of God in Stan's ministry. The story of Stan and John becomes for us the story of God's faithfulness and our prayer—the essential response to God.

Santiago Atitlán

When Peter and I arrived in Guatemala City, John was
at the airport to welcome us. He stayed with us until we left
ten days later. After a day in the city we made the long trip
to Santiago Atitlán. As Peter and I commented on the beauty
of the landscape, John kept saying, "Ah, this is nothing
compared with what you are going to see." And indeed I will
never forget the moment the road made a turn and opened
up a spectacular view of Lake Atitlán, surrounded by
volcanoes wrapped with fast-moving clouds, and decorated
on its edges with small towns shining like bright jewels on a
golden ring. Peter and I had seen many other lakes, but
somehow this vision of majesty and gentle beauty fixed itself
on our minds. "There, at the end of that inlet, is Santiago,"
said John, pointing to the other side of the lake. "You can't
see it from here because it lies hidden behind the 'Cerro de
Oro' or 'golden hill.' But we will soon be there and you will
be even more impressed than you are now!"

Thirty minutes later we left the blacktop road and started the last stretch of our journey over a narrow, bumpy gravel road which winds itself in endless curves between the corn-fields, and here and there offers a distant view of the lake. "I seldom make it home without getting sick on this road," John said as he tried to steer his Bronco between the big holes in front of us. "But don't worry, you will be rewarded for this *via dolorosa*."

A panoramic view of Lake Atitlán greets visitors.

Indeed we were. As we finally entered the town of Santiago, we found ourselves surrounded by many friendly men, women and children in colorful clothes. We drove slowly through the tiny streets, passed the busy marketplace, and came to the central square by a stately old colonial church. We left the Bronco, walked up the church steps, and marveled at the view from the porch. Around us lay the little town of Santiago; beyond its houses and huts the glistening lake was dotted with fishing boats, and beyond the lake the mountain slopes soared up, covered with forest and corn-fields. "Well, what do you think?" asked John. "It is so beautiful, peaceful and friendly, so far away from New York and Boston," I responded, trying to express what I felt. "Welcome to Santiago. I'm glad you made it," John said with a generous smile. "You will see many things, some holy and some evil, some good and some bad, some beautiful and some ugly. Not everything is as lovely as what you see before you now. This may look like paradise, but it certainly is not paradise yet." We knew something of this truth from reading about Guatemala, but we needed to be reminded. "Let's go into the house," John said. "First, I want to show you the place most dear to me."

A village sidestreet leads to the cloud-enshrouded volcano.

*S*tan's Room

We entered the large building that was a combination rectory, convent and clinic. Wherever we went we met people, running back and forth, playing, waiting to receive medicine, scrubbing floors, washing clothes, preparing a meal, or just chatting and laughing. So many new faces, colors and sounds. "Who are all these people? What are they here for? What are they talking about? What does this all mean?" John noticed our puzzlement. "Just relax . . . don't worry . . . just follow me." Suddenly, we found ourselves in a small room, in the heart of the house. Here it was quiet, in stark contrast to the many sounds we had just passed through. It was a very ordinary room. In one corner, a tabernacle stood surrounded by a few candles, two vases with large flowers, and a pedestal with a statue of the Blessed Virgin. There were a few old chairs and some cushions on the floor. Against the wall behind the tabernacle a large poster and some smaller photographs were pinned. I recognized the pictures of the former Archbishop of San Salvador Oscar Romero and Sister Ita Ford, two victims of Salvadoran death squads in 1980. On the other wall three large portraits were hung. Two stately portraits of American bishops flanked a large picture of Stan, a bearded man, casually dressed, with a sturdy face and gentle eyes. We knelt down on the floor and prayed for a while. We knew where we were. I had a hard time knowing how I felt. It seemed that sadness and joy, agony and victory, despair and hope all merged in this simple prayer room.

The room where Stan Rother was murdered is now a parish chapel.

After a few moments John said, "This is the room where they murdered him. Look here under the tabernacle on the floor. You can see the bullet hole of one of the bullets which killed him. . . . And here, look, you can still see the stain of his blood on the wall. It must have been an awful struggle." I looked again at the portrait of the man: an Oklahoma farmer, priest, martyr . . . brutally murdered in the early morning hours of July 28, 1981.

Peter, John and I just stood there for a while, looking at this most ordinary place that filled us with a strange feeling of awe. I felt less anger toward the three men who had killed him than gratitude toward the one who had lived in this house for 13 years and stayed here to the bitter but some-how glorious end. It was not hard for me to let the words come: "Pray for us, Stan, pray for us now and at the hour of our death." After a long silence John said:

> The first time I walked into this room, I knew something was wrong. It wasn't a room meant for socializing. Then one evening while I prayed with our sisters, an inspiration hit me. I talked with the sisters and they thought it was a great idea: We made the room where Stan was mar-tyred into a chapel. We couldn't have done a better thing. We knew that here, where he was martyred, we had to come together to pray. I could not understand why for three years the room had remained empty and unused. For some reason, it became obvious to us that this should be the place where we praise God for all the great things he has done and is doing among his people, thank him for Stan's life and death, and ask him for the strength and courage to continue his ministry of love and reconciliation among the people.

From the moment Stan's room was made into a small
chapel, John and the Carmelite sisters who had continued
Stan's ministry after his death came together three times
a day to pray. As they entered Stan's room to pray one
morning at six o'clock, John suddenly had to laugh. It came
to him that more than 20 years earlier at Mount St. Mary's
Seminary in Emmitsburg, Maryland, Stan and John had
come together to pray at the same early hour. It struck him
as humorous that they should meet again in this room and in
this way after 20 years.

For John there are few coincidences in life. Every event,
for him, is part of God's mysterious plan. One must just pay
attention and listen carefully to the movement of the Spirit.
God had brought John and Stan together for just one year in
the seminary. That had been enough to awaken in John the
deep desire to take Stan's place when he heard of his
sudden death. As John stood in the little room and looked at
the bullet hole and the bloodstains, he knew he was called to
be in Santiago Atitlán. Stan's faithfulness was John's hope;
Stan's death was John's life. Stan's witness became John's
courage to continue the work with the people of Santiago.
Tertullian once wrote: "The blood of the martyrs is the seed
of the church." Stan had sown the seed; John had come to
reap the harvest.

A few days after visiting the new chapel I read the
sermon preached by Bishop Angelico Melotto in the church
of Santiago Atitlán on September 3, 1981, at a memorial
Mass for Stan. His words strengthened my growing
conviction that somehow I had been allowed to glimpse the
mysterious ways in which God guides his people. Bishop
Melotto said:

The planting of the Church in Guatemala was
not done, as in other parts of the world, by the
shedding of blood. Now the time of martyrdom
has come also to the Church of Guatemala.
The priests, religious, catechists and ministers of
the word who have fallen victim to the violence
of these latest times are the modern martyrs of
the . . . Church who will be remembered in the
history of the Church of Guatemala and will be
its brightest glory. . . .

It won't be long before our Father
Francisco [Stanley] will . . . be recognized by
the highest authority of the Church as a true
martyr of Christ. . . . The Church does not
prohibit us from asking his intercession for us,
so that we might receive what we need. Let us
all, therefore, ask him for the grace to soon
have again in this parish community good
priests who, following his example, will
continue his work. Alleluia! (Quoted from *The
Sooner Catholic*, October 11, 1981).

As I let these words sink in, I saw clearly how deeply the
lives of Stan and John were interconnected. This connection
was not built on their casual encounter of a few years ago,
nor simply on a desire to take a martyr's place, but on three
years of fervent prayer by the people of Santiago Atitlán to
their martyred priest. John knew this, and he was therefore
not merely pious when he invited me with the words: "I want
you to come here and pray with me and my people."

The six days that Peter and I stayed with John in
Santiago Atitlán were filled with moving and joyful as well as
sorrowful experiences. We prayed with John and the sisters,
celebrated splendid liturgies, witnessed the funeral services of
three small children, attended meetings with eucharistic
ministers and catechists, made a short retreat in a nearby
retreat house, visited a neighboring parish, walked and
jogged through the streets of Santiago, and ate many tortillas
and beans. But when we came home, none of these activities
seemed as important as the encounter with two men, who
through their death and life embody the story of God's
faithfulness to his people and the true meaning of a life of
prayer. This is the reason their stories must be told.

*F*or Christ in His People

Behind the main altar in the large colonial church, built by Franciscans around 1550, Stan's heart and a piece of gauze saturated with his blood are buried. While Stan's family chose to have him buried in Oklahoma, they allowed his heart and some of his blood to remain in Santiago Atitlán. The stone that covers the grave reads: "Father Stanley Francisco Rother, Priest and Martyr." Every time I entered the church I noticed people praying at Stan's grave. Often their prayers were so loud that they soared up to the high spaces of the nave. John told me that on the night of July 28th, not an hour passed without a large group of people kneeling around Stan's grave. It may be years, decades or even centuries before the church officially declares Stan a saint, but the people of Santiago Atitlán are not waiting.

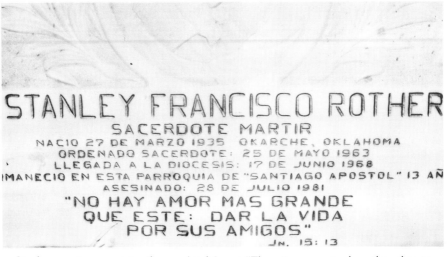

STANLEY FRANCISCO ROTHER
SACERDOTE MARTIR
NACIO 27 DE MARZO 1935 OKARCHE, OKLAHOMA
ORDENADO SACERDOTE: 25 DE MAYO 1963
LLEGADA A LA DIOCESIS: 17 DE JUNIO 1968
IMANECIO EN ESTA PARROQUIA DE "SANTIAGO APOSTOL" 13 AÑ
ASESINADO: 28 DE JULIO 1981
"NO HAY AMOR MAS GRANDE
QUE ESTE: DAR LA VIDA
POR SUS AMIGOS"
JN. 15:13

Stan's gravestone contains the words of Jesus: "There is no greater love than this: to lay down one's life for one's friends."

They have already declared Padre Francisco—whom they call
"A'plas" in their native language—a saint. They come to him
daily and ask for help with their concrete, personal needs.
He is one of them, a father, brother and friend who for 13
years served them on earth and now intercedes for them in
heaven. They know God will hear his pleas for a poor,
oppressed and malnourished people. Padre Francisco taught,
fed, healed, prayed with and cared for them in the past; he
will certainly care for them now. He was their shepherd, he
still is their shepherd.

Close to the altar was a large photograph of Stan.
Whenever John pointed to it during a homily people paid
special attention. They wanted to hear again what "Padre
A'plas" told them years ago. They wanted to be reminded of
him and strengthened by his memory. Their heads nodded
approvingly when they heard his words recalled, as if saying:
"Yes, that is what he told us; we must not forget."

Who was this man to whom the Tzutuhíl Indians of
Santiago Atitlán pray every day, whose words are
remembered with great fondness and whose picture is
regarded with deep gratitude and love? When Bishop Melotto
predicted that Stan would eventually be recognized by the
highest authority of the church as a true martyr, he said:
"Those who suffer martyrdom in these times will be
remembered in history as Martyrs of Human Promotion,
because all human beings are made in the image of God and
are our brothers and sisters in Christ" (*The Sooner Catholic*,
October 11, 1981). This sentence offers a clue to Stan's
unique sanctity. He was not thrown to the lions like the early
Christians for refusing to worship a god other than the God
of Jesus Christ. He was not tortured and killed like the early
missionaries in Japan who refused to trample the image of

the crucified Christ. Stan was killed because he was faithful to his people in their long and painful struggle for human dignity. He stood with them as they learned how to read and write, sought proper nutrition and health care for their children, struggled to acquire small pieces of land to cultivate, and gradually freed themselves from the chains of poverty and oppression.

Stan was a martyr of human promotion, a man killed because his unrelenting care for poor and tired people became a threat to those who resist any change in the existing order, an order in which the rich hide behind walls and the poor beg for food to survive. Stan was a martyr for the living Christ, the Christ who lives among the poor. In one of his last letters, written on July 13, 1981, he quoted Jesus' words: "When I was hungry you gave me to eat; when I was thirsty you gave me to drink," and added, "this is one of my favorite scripture quotations and I often use it. . . ." Stan was a martyr for his people, in whom he recognized the face of the suffering Christ.

Some who read about his death may think he was a hapless victim of political upheaval in Guatemala. They may conclude he was at the wrong place at the wrong time, and that his faith in Jesus, his priesthood and his own inner convictions had little to do with his death. They may even consider it preposterous to view him as a martyr for Christ and a saint of the church. But those who respond in this way do not recognize the new form of martyrdom emerging in the church of Central America in our time. It is martyrdom— witness—to the living Christ present in his people. Stan's martyrdom, like that of Archbishop Romero, Ita Ford and her companions, and countless others who consciously refuse to abandon their faith, reveals to us in a new way the great mystery of the church as the body of Christ. Stan died for his people, and for and with Christ. The same Christ who died on the cross and rose on the third day continues to unfold among his people the inexhaustible depth of God's love. Christ gathers into himself all humanity—past, present and future. Wherever or whenever people suffer and search for new life, the mystery of God's salvation through Christ becomes manifest again.

It is this mystery, which is the mystery of the church, the people of God, that is reaffirmed by the martyrdom of Stan Rother. Stan's death, like that of Christ himself, took place within a certain political context. Each time we confess, "He suffered and died under Pontius Pilate," we are reminded of the political context of our faith. It was precisely in the concreteness of human history, with its power struggles and socioeconomic tensions, that God chose to reveal his love and continues to do so. But when we try to explain the mystery of God's salvation by pointing to the political and socioeconomic tensions of our time, we are like people who blame a war on the presence of arms. Stan's martyrdom is first and foremost a spiritual event, an event through which the Spirit of God breaks into history. The political context reminds us that God indeed became flesh and lived among us in the often gruesome concreteness of our daily existence.

Photo of Stan Rother by Frankie Williams.

A Quiet Giant

I have never met Stan Rother personally. All I know of him I know from John Vesey, from the Carmelite sisters who lived with him, from the members of his parish, from 22 letters written during the last year of his life, and from articles published in *The Sooner Catholic* in the months after his death. Stan emerges from these sources as a solid, down-to-earth, gentle, caring, hardworking, good natured Oklahoma farmer. John vividly remembers his first meeting with Stan. It was on the basketball court of the seminary.

> Here I was, a kid from the streets of Brooklyn running into this sturdy midwesterner from Oklahoma. He really didn't know how to play basketball, and he beat the daylights out of me. He kept apologizing every time he hit me. But I just couldn't get angry at him. His face so expressed the pain he felt when he fouled me. He was a man built like a steel rod with a wiry strength, but he was very, very gentle. It was this gentleness that diffused my anger.

The words "strong" and "gentle" appear often in the descriptions of Stan by family and friends. The most moving description comes from Father Robert Silverman who said: "His eyes were the eyes of a gentle, gentle person. Such a beautiful man. Violence was as far from him as the earth is from the moon. He was a quiet man though not a wallflower type at all. He was a quiet giant. He was there when you needed him. Unsung. He was a man who knew what he was all about" (*The Sooner Catholic*, August 16, 1981). Stan's sister affirms this beautiful portrait when she says: "He was a quiet person. But when he had a job to do, he did it completely. He never left anything unfinished." And to this she adds a gift that Stan shares with John: "When he laughed, he caught you up in his joy. He laughed so hard, you had to laugh too" (*Ibid.*).

In my mind's eye I see a wiry Sooner striding the streets of Santiago, sharing the joys and sorrows of his people, enjoying especially those moments of laughter that bind us all together. He was the tough, strong servant of God who would never break a "bruised reed" but who was unafraid to promote justice. His photograph reveals his gentle eyes, his letters speak his care for the people, and his friends witness to his unceasing efforts on behalf of human dignity.

A Busy Parish

In June 1968, after having fulfilled various pastoral tasks in his home diocese, Stan was appointed to the mission team at Santiago Atitlán by Bishop Victor J. Reed. Four years earlier, the Oklahoma City-Tulsa Diocese had sent some of its priests to the newly created Diocese of Sololá in Guatemala and accepted full responsibility for Santiago Atitlán, the oldest parish in that diocese. In his memorial sermon for Stan, Bishop Melotto refers to these early years:

> The first group of priests, headed by the Reverend Ramon Carlin . . . arrived with great enthusiasm and abundant material support, and began immediately to work toward the realization of the great plans they had made under the name "Micatokla" (Catholic Mission of Oklahoma). This was cause for great joy for all the people of Atitlán. Shortly after the first missioners came from Oklahoma, the young priest Stanley Francis Rother arrived. He was destined to crown the pastoral activities of Micatokla with the shedding of his own blood" (*The Sooner Catholic*, October 11, 1981).

When Stan arrived in Santiago in 1968 at the age of 33, he found plenty of work to do. Many of his people were chronically hungry. Though in the summer the fields are rich with corn, beans and squash, and though September brings forth more avocados than you can count, the Tzutuhíl Indians hardly profit from the wealth around them. Some own a small plot of land that gives them a little food, while others depend on the low pay they receive from the land-owner for whom they work; having enough work to make a living remains uncertain from day to day and from week to week. With at least 34,000 people in Santiago, countless people are undernourished. Sister Guadeloupe runs a dispensary and sees hundreds of Tzutuhíl Indians every week. When I asked her what the main health problem is, she did not hesitate for a moment: "Malnutrition, which makes people susceptible to all sorts of illnesses and causes many deaths, especially of babies and young children."

I saw how right she was. During the days Peter and I were in Santiago we saw the funerals of three children under the age of two. There is also the problem of illiteracy. Very few people can speak, read or write Spanish and even fewer can read or write in their own Tzutuhíl language. There is the problem of shelter. Large families often have to live in a one-room hut with a thatched roof. They cook, eat, sleep and often work in the same place. Is it surprising that the little clinic in town gives out many tranquilizers?

Of course, the pastor must also perform baptisms, marriages and funerals, prepare countless young people for first communion and confirmation, train and guide catechists and eucharistic ministers, and visit the sick, elderly and dying. Daily, people are at the door who have nothing to eat, no money to go to town, no way to find a doctor, no decent clothes, no place to call home. I have not even mentioned the Sunday Masses to which about 3,500 people come, and the many Masses in the small communities in the area, far away from the town and hard to reach.

With so much to do, so many people to help and so many places to visit, no one working in Santiago Atitlán would ever feel that the task was finished. There always remains a sense of hardly touching the roots of the problems, of never having the time to do a job well, of seldom having the chance to quietly reflect on the complexities of the situation. The life of a priest in Santiago Atitlán is constantly interrupted and mostly dominated by urgencies and emergencies.

Stan worked in this context with all of his talents. Together with his co-workers he tried to respond to the ever-present physical, emotional and spiritual needs of his people.

Always the quiet one, he never seemed flustered or overwhelmed by the situation. His strong, steady character made
him work day in, day out with calm perseverance and firm
commitment to the people. He didn't expect quick changes.
He just wanted to be there with his people and do whatever
he could. After three years in the parish, he wrote on a form
for the personnel board of his archdiocese under the heading
"Remarks": "Plan to stay here for some time." This dry
understatement reveals a character that hated dramatization
and knew that patience was the way.

One of the most remarkable aspects of Stan's ministry in
Santiago was his mastery of the difficult Tzutuhíl language.
This is most surprising since Stan was not known to be a
good student during his seminary years. In fact, he was
dropped from the Assumption Seminary in San Antonio,
Texas, because of his poor academic work. Had it not been
for Father Edmund Von Elm and Bishop Victor J. Reed,
who saw more in him than most of his professors and
sent him to Mount St. Mary's Seminary, he never would
have become a priest. Stan's devotion to his people gave him
the motivation to learn a language more difficult than any he
was required to learn in the seminary.

In 1974, after six years in the parish, Stan was named
administrator of the Oklahoma mission. The years that
followed saw different priests come and go; by 1980, Stan
found himself working with only one other priest, a
Guatemalan Indian named Pedro Bocel. But at just that time
he was blessed by the arrival of a group of sisters who
offered their help to the parish. In his Christmas letter of
1980 he wrote:

In early May I had the pleasant surprise of a group of religious that actually came and asked for a place to work. After some quick arrangements and stretching the permission a little, they moved into their convent in early September. They are seven professed Indian Sisters, Missionary Carmelites of St. Teresa, along with a Mexican Sister and a Guatemalan as directors. Most of their work will be with the women, the girls, the sick, literacy training, catechism, liturgical music, banners, etc. . . .

Sister Sylvia

Reading this now, the coming of the sisters seems like a divine preparation for Stan's martyrdom. Seven months after this was written Stan was dead and his associate Pedro Bocel had fled to the United States to save his life. After Stan's death, the sisters were ready to take over the parish and attend to the pastoral needs of the people for three years.

Increasing Violence

In September 1980, the political situation in Guatemala had worsened so much that Stan realized his own life and those of his people and co-workers were in danger. People suspected of being "subversives" or being sympathetic to the revolutionary cause were being kidnapped, tortured and brutally murdered. The violence took on demonic proportions. Whole villages were being destroyed and the people massacred or forcibly moved. Thousands of Indians fled their homes. Often it was hard to tell if people were in hiding or had been kidnapped and killed.

In his many letters during this period, letters not mailed but carried to the United States by visitors, Stan gives us some idea of the way he experienced the increasing tension and how he tried to live with it. His first concern remained his colleague Pedro. He realized that if the government would not allow him as a foreigner to stay in Guatemala, the life of his Indian associate would be in danger. This is the reason he tried to get a visa for Pedro. To his archbishop in Oklahoma Stan wrote:

I do not intend to leave him here to be killed if I have to leave, or if we see that he is in imminent danger. I want to get him out of the country. He was just ordained in January and I feel that he should not have to be sacrificed so early in his ministry (September 22, 1980).

Stan Rother and Father Pedro Bocel, an assistant at Santiago Atitlán.

While Stan's letters express in many different ways his
deep conviction that he should stay with his people as long
as possible and not leave them unless there was no choice,
he did everything possible to protect the life of Pedro. Here
again Stan showed great courage when he thought of himself
and great prudence and care when he thought of others. His
desire to obtain a visa for Pedro, which required the help of
his archbishop in the United States, offered an occasion to
explain the situation in Santiago Atitlán in more detail. In a
long letter to Archbishop Charles Salatka of Oklahoma City,
he offered a vivid picture of the general tensions in the
country and the particular tensions in his parish:

The country here is in rebellion and the government is taking it out on the Church. The low wages that are paid, the very few who are excessively rich, the bad distribution of land—these are some of the reasons for widespread discontent. The Church seems to be the only force that is trying to do something about the situation, and therefore the government is after us. There are some that say the Diocese of Sololá, where this mission is, is the next area on the list for persecution. . . .

Here in Atitlán, we are very cautious. The army was here in force during the fiesta the latter part of July, dressed in camouflage fatigues and carrying submachine guns. They didn't do anything but put everyone on edge, walking around in groups of three or four, standing on the corners watching everything. Since then we have had strangers in town, asking questions about the priests, this catechist or that one, where they live, who is in charge of the Cooperative, who are the leaders, etc. Because of this intimidation, several of the leaders of the different organizations are out of town or in hiding. It has changed our style of life here in the rectory too. The doors and gates are being made more secure, the front door is now locked all the time, and people just can't enter at will. These twelve years I have slept in the same room that overlooks the plaza in front of the church, but since a rectory and convent were attacked with grenades in the eastern part of the country, I sleep elsewhere now, where the walls are rock instead of wood (*Ibid.*).

A quiet realism pervades this letter: no exaggeration, dramatization, panic or overconfidence. With a certain objective distance, Stan tries to give his archbishop an honest picture of his situation and to evaluate carefully the nature of the danger he and his people are exposed to. Even though he keeps himself out of all politics and wants only to be a pastor to his people, he cannot ignore the fact that educating and forming his people in the faith also opens their eyes to the larger context in which they have to live out their faith. In the same letter he wrote:

> I am aware that some of our younger catechists are working with those that are preparing for a revolution. They are young men who are becoming more and more conscious of their situation and are convinced that the only option for them is revolt. The more unrest and action against the government, the more the government is pushing repression (*Ibid.*).

*T*he Good Shepherd

In 1980 that repression came closer and closer to Santiago Atitlán. Levelheaded Stan knew that he had to be extremely careful; he realized that he had to take all possible measures to protect the people, the sisters, the catechists and other co-workers, his associate Father Pedro, and himself. But he also knew that he had to stay with his people as long as possible. He wrote:

> The reality is that we are in danger. But we don't know when or what form the government will use to further repress the Church. For a month or so now, all classes and group meetings have been cancelled. We are working in smaller groups. My associate and myself are seen less on the street, and almost never leave the rectory at night. The tactic of the government has been to kidnap those they think are leaders, torture and then kill them. Two days ago a young man from the neighboring parish was taken in the middle of the night. He is a cousin of one of our nuns. He is not expected to be found alive (*Ibid.*).

Fifty-five percent of the Guatemalan population is Indian. These indigenous people, like the native Americans and blacks in the United States, have occupied the lowest level in society. The racist contempt that they have traditionally suffered makes them easy scapegoats and the first victims of government repression. Recognizing this reality, Stan worried much about his Guatemalan Indian associate, Father Pedro Bocel. Yet, because of his status as a U.S. citizen, he still considered himself rather safe.

> I am not in as much danger as he [Pedro] is, because I am a foreigner, and I hope they will give me a chance of leaving if they want me out. They haven't killed an American priest *yet* (*Ibid.*).

Parishioners carry the caskets at the funeral of two children.

Before he finished this letter, however, Stan made it clear to his archbishop in a very understated way that he was ready to offer his life for his people. He knew he had a way out—returning to the United States where he would be safe—but the many years in Santiago created a bond with his people that he did not want to break. The thought of abandoning his people repulsed him.

> If I get a direct threat or am told to leave, then I will go. But if it is my destiny that I should give my life here, then so be it. . . . I don't want to desert these people, and that is what will be said, even after all these years. There is still a lot of good that can be done under the circumstances. . . . Pray for us that we may continue to serve as best we can in the reality where we find ourselves (*Ibid.*).

This letter reveals much. Most of all, it shows a great humility that hesitates to use the many biblical images that so easily come to mind. What would have been easier for a priest who wrote to his bishop than to quote John 15:13: "A man can have no greater love than to lay down his life for his friends." There was a reluctance in his letters to use lofty words for his own situation. While his solid commitment to stay with his people became stronger as the months went by, his thoughts about his own vocation remained simply stated. Occasionally his humor surfaced even in the face of increasing tension. The only time he mentioned martyrdom was to quote a fellow priest from a neighboring parish who said to him: "I like martyrs, but just to read about them." However, the biblical image that emerged as he approached the day of his death was the image of the good shepherd who does not abandon his sheep. He did not mention such thoughts to his bishop in September 1980, but soon after that, to his friend Frankie Williams, he wrote:

> At the first signs of danger, the shepherd can't run and leave the sheep to fend for themselves. I heard about a couple of nuns in Nicaragua who left during the fighting and later wanted to go back. The people asked them, "Where were you when we needed you?" They couldn't stay and were forced to leave. I don't want that to happen to me. I have too much of my life invested here to run (November 16, 1980).

He wrote this in November. The Christmas season brought
more violence. Several people were kidnapped, and the
authorities paid informers to identify more "communists."
Wives and children were left without husbands and fathers;
fear started to dominate the daily life of the community. Stan
realized that some in his own parish were criticizing him, but
he saw it as a sign that he was doing the right thing. He
wrote:

> A nice compliment was given to me recently
> when a supposed leader in the Church and
> town was complaining that "Father is defending
> the people." He wants me deported for my sin
> (1980 Christmas letter).

And with this dangerous compliment in mind he returned to
the image of the good shepherd, whose love is stronger than
his fear.

> This is one of the reasons I have for staying in
> the face of physical harm. The shepherd cannot
> run at the first sign of danger. Pray for us that
> we may be a sign of the love of Christ for our
> people, that our presence among them will
> fortify them to endure these sufferings in
> preparation for the coming of the Kingdom
> (*Ibid.*).

*F*ears and Smiles

Living in a difficult and dangerous situation is often easier than living with the awareness that someone you love dearly is in danger and you can do little about it. Stan's family read the horrible stories about what was going on in Guatemala, yet received only sporadic news about him. They must have suffered more than Stan himself during these months. In a letter to his sister on November 25, 1980, Stan described his awareness of the agonies he caused his family.

> Rumors . . . get out of hand and when one can't have direct contact . . . it just makes the whole thing worse. The Archbishop [in the U.S.A.] called the Bishop here [in Sololá] on Friday and insisted on talking to me personally. The Bishop sent his driver over here on Saturday morning to tell me about it, and in the afternoon I drove to Panajachel to call him. I forgot to tell him to give the folks a ring, and it really didn't seem necessary to call them at the time. It wasn't until Tuesday that I found a note at the Maryknoll House [in Guatemala City] that you all had called. Mother started to cry when she recognized my voice and then I realized what you all had been through.

As long as you are in the midst of the situation and can respond to the concrete events of the day, you can control your own fear and anxiety. But when you are a great distance from it, and know vaguely what is happening but are totally powerless to do anything about it, your fears come devastatingly close. That is the reason parents often suffer so intensely for the sake of their children far away. Stan's parents and family must have gone through many agonizing moments in this time of distant rumor, half-truths, sensational news reports, and piecemeal information about their son and brother.

Meanwhile, Stan himself seemed to be in very good spirits. He certainly did not lose his sense of humor. His response to "the tabernacle thief" shows this clearly. To his friends Joe and Mary he wrote:

> I was amused about your not liking the tabernacle being moved over to the side. Our sisters had a night-time visitor a couple of weeks ago, and he crawled into the first floor through a window into the chapel. . . . He left with the tabernacle under his arm and two or three small statues. Two sisters sleeping on the first floor didn't hear him, but some on the second did. For our luck, we had lost the key to the tabernacle door and the pyx [small box containing consecrated hosts] fell out and was recovered the next morning. The first floor windows now have bars (December 17, 1980).

Stan's unsentimental and dry response to this sacrilegious event certainly shows that he is a different kind of saint. So does his response to an involuntary holiday fast:

> My Thanksgiving dinner this year wasn't what I had planned. I had received an invitation to eat at San Lucas [the neighboring parish with priests and sisters from New Ulm, Minnesota] and intended to do so, but didn't get back from the City in time and had to go into Cerro de Oro for Mass at 5 p.m. I came back here and had a bread and peanut butter sandwich while my stomach was expecting turkey (*Ibid.*).

Photo of Stan Rother by Frankie Williams.

Hardworking, down-to-earth, undramatic, with a self-effacing sense of humor and great dedication to his people—these are the qualities that emerge from the letters which Stan sends to his family and friends. Reading these letters three and a half years after his death I am impressed by Stan's inner strength during a period of mounting danger. Though he joked about the night visitor and his peanut butter sandwich for Thanksgiving, he also wrote about the increasing violence around him.

> Just a month ago now we had four that were taken in four days. The people were terrorized and hundreds took refuge in the church at night just for mutual protection. We had a couple of guys stay with us at night too to keep watch and let us know if we were in grave danger. Since then the radio [station] has been rifled and some of the equipment has been taken. The director was the third one to go. . . . Two weeks ago another was taken and last Friday another was buried here. He is the first to have been found. Two others are missing who probably were with the last one, and I got a rumor today where I might find them alive (hopefully) (November 25, 1980).

In another letter, after writing about the same events he added:

> Father Pedro and I have been afraid like everyone else, but we are fine . . . we have no direct information that we are being sought . . . many of the leaders in town are in hiding in other parts of the country. It is a shame that this has to happen, but it is part of a process going on in these parts of the world. I guess we will get used to it little by little (November 16, 1980).

*T*error at His Doorstep

Shortly after New Year's Day, terror came to his doorstep. He witnessed the kidnapping of one of his most beloved and competent catechists. In a heart-rending letter, which was reprinted in the *New York Times* a few weeks after his death, he wrote a friend:

> Things have been pretty quiet the past couple of weeks until last Saturday night. Probably the most sought-after catechist had been staying here in the rectory off and on, and almost constantly of late. He had been eating and sleeping here and usually visiting his wife and two kids in late afternoon. He had a key to the house, and as he was approaching Saturday night about 7:45 he was intercepted by a group of four kidnappers. Three apparently tried to grab him at the far side of the church as he approached on the porch that fronts the Catholic Action offices, the church and the rectory. He got to within fifteen feet of the door

and was holding on to the bannister and yelling for help. The other priest [Pedro] heard the ruckus outside and stepped out to see them trying to take him. He considered trying to help, but was scared by their height. He called me from the living room where I was listening to music but also heard the noise, and by the time I realized what was happening, grabbed a jacket and got outside, they had taken him down the front steps of the church and were putting him in a waiting car. In the process they had broken the bannister where the rectory porch joins the church, and I just stood there wanting to jump down to help, but knowing that I would be killed or taken along also. The car sped off with him yelling for help, but no one able to do so. Then I realized that Fr. Pedro, Frankie Williams from Wichita, and I had just witnessed a kidnapping of someone that we had gotten to know and love and were unable to do anything about it. They had his mouth covered, but I can still hear his muffled screams for help. As I got back in the rectory I got a cramp in my back from the anger I felt that this friend was being taken off to be tortured for a day or two and then brutally murdered for wanting a better life and more justice for his people. He had told me before, "I have never stolen, have never hurt anyone, have never eaten someone else's food, why then do they want to hurt me and kill me?"

Sunday morning we heard that all the passengers of the late bus from the city heard the kidnapped yelling for help as they met the four-door sedan led by a military jeep and followed by a military ambulance. . . . He was thirty years old, left a wife and two boys, ages three and one. May he rest in peace!

About twenty minutes after the kidnapping,
I went to the telephone office and asked the
police in San Lucas to investiage a car coming
their way. I told them it was a kidnapping
and that they were armed. They said they
would see about it, but they proably hid
instead. We heard yesterday that four or
possibly five were kidnapped there that same
night. Coming back from the call, I was
informed that a fragmentation grenade was
found in front of the church. It was probably
dropped during the scuffling.

That makes eleven members of this
community that have been kidnapped and all
are presumed dead. Only one body has been
positively identified and buried here; there are
possibly three buried in a common grave in
Chimaltenango. They were picked up in
Antigua and the following week I went to all
the hospitals and morgues in the area and got a
list of their characteristics and clothing (January
5, 1981).

I am struck by the restraint with which Stan told this terrifying
story. He described events in precise detail, yet hardly
mentioned his own feelings. We get just a glimpse of his own
agony when he noted the back cramp caused by the anger
he felt from seeing a friend taken away to be tortured and
murdered. But it is precisely this "holy distance" from the
violence that surrounded him that allowed him not to run off
in panic, but stay with his people and tend to their daily
increasing needs. Instead of being overwhelmed by the dark
forces that were closing in, he tried to help those who were
left without husband or father. He wrote:

For these eleven that are gone, there are eight
widows and thirty-two children among the
group. These people are going to need
emergency help. Others have had to flee also
to save their lives and to find work in exile is
almost impossible. They will also need help.
Some of these have had salaries in the radio,
artisan coops, health promoter, etc., and
haven't been engaged in subsistence farming.
They will need time to find other means of
income, and for the widows with children, this
will be extremely difficult. Letters asking for
help are on their way right now to London
. . . and they will very likely send some money.
This was organized by someone else and I
accepted the task of funneling the money to
where it is needed . . . helping these people
could very easily be considered subversive by
the local government . . . (*Ibid.*).

*S*ubversive Service

This last sentence contains the key to the unique quality of Stan's martyrdom. Stan came as a pastor, a shepherd, to Santiago Atitlán, and he remained a pastor to the very end. He stayed far from politics and politicians, but he never allowed politics or politicians to interfere with his primary task: caring for his people. Without wanting or deserving it, Stan's pastoral commitment increasingly made him an enemy of those who had power. In the context of the struggle of the poor for dignity, lending a hand to an Indian peasant becomes a political act. Stan knew that. That is why he said: "helping these people could very easily be considered subversive." If that is subversive then Stan was willing to take the risk—although with many precautions—to be considered as such. The political situation causes immense violence, the violence causes deep human suffering, and the suffering calls for pastoral care and healing—independent of who is to blame. It was this care for the people, at all times and in all circumstances, that would lead to the deaths of Archbishop Oscar Romero, Ita Ford and many others. It would also be the true source of Stan's martyrdom.

After describing the brutal kidnapping of his beloved catechist, Stan reaffirmed his commitment to stay.

I am not ready to call it quits yet. What
happened last Saturday was indeed scary and
happened at our doorstep, but we don't know
if his [the catechist's] presence here with us will
affect us directly. We have not received any
direct or anonymous threats, nor are there
rumors that we are considered imminent
targets. . . . Other towns in the Diocese are
being hit harder than us at present. In the past
couple of months three priests of the Diocese
had to leave because of direct threats, and two
others got scared and left. All but one were
foreigners (*Ibid.*).

Although Stan did not analyze the political situation, and seldom went into depth about the revolutionary movements in the region, he was convinced that his people had little choice but to revolt. He never condoned violence. On the contrary, he condemned it in all its forms. But he also understood that the uprising of his people was a desperate response to centuries of repression. He wrote:

> This whole Central American area is in the process of change, and if the governments don't want to do it peacefully, then it will be done by war. It is sad but it has to happen. . . . Just say a prayer on occasion that we will be safe and still able to be of service to these people of God (*Ibid.*).

*O*n the Death List

Stan wrote this on January 5, 1981. Two days later, 16 people were massacred at Chacaya, a coffee plantation near Santiago Atitlán. A few days after the massacre, a friend of Stan was informed by a government source that Stan's name had appeared on a death list. At the time, Stan was in Guatemala City on parish business. After much telephoning, the friend was able to get the message to Stan advising him to get out of the country as soon as possible. Now a direct threat had appeared, Stan had become an "imminent target," and he was no longer safe in Santiago, nor anywhere else in Guatemala. Staying would have been suicidal. On January 29th Stan was back with his family in Oklahoma.

It is important to see that Stan's willingness to give his life for his people did not mean that he wanted to be killed. There was no desire for heroism, no daredevil gestures; not even a hope for martyrdom. Any of that would have been totally out of character for Stan Rother. He was a prudent man who loved life and wanted to live as long as possible.

His people were his first concern, but he was willing to leave
them when no chance to live with them presented itself. He
had written to his archbishop: "If I get a direct threat, then I
will go" (September 22, 1980). The threat came and he left.
There was no other choice for a prudent man. As soon as
Stan arrived home he was urged to become active in
solidarity work for Central America and bombarded with
requests to speak about Guatemala. With Pedro he attended
a workshop in Mexico, and occasionally he gave a speech,
but overall he was hesitant to become involved in new
activities. His overriding desire was to return to his people.
He was not yet ready to remain in the United States and do
solidarity work and lecturing. In his heart he no longer felt at
home in the United States. He had become so close to his
people that Santiago had become his true home. He wanted
only one thing: to return to Guatemala as soon as he could.
To Brother Mark Gruenke, a Christian Brother, he wrote on
March 3, 1981:

> After working there for twelve and a half years,
> I feel almost like a Guatemalan and I still want
> to return.

But was it safe to return? That became the haunting
question. He realized the risks and weighed his chances:

> I want to return soon, but then I might not be
> given the chance to escape again. . . . Ten
> days ago I called back and the government
> source that told us we were threatened said we
> could now go back. The big question is—
> should I take a chance and go back? Nobody
> has yet convinced me to stay here (*Ibid.*).

*O*ne Accusation
I Don't Want

He took the risk, and by Holy Week Stan was back with his people in Santiago Atitlán. Pedro also returned to Guatemala but for safety reasons went to another diocese. Stan was now the only priest in the parish. Although he wrote to his friends: "Things seem to be calm" (June 1), and "Things are looking up around here" (July 11), the feeling of being unsafe remained with him. In May he returned for a few days to the United States to attend the ordination and first Mass of his cousin, Don Wolf. When writing Don on June 1st, he hinted at his anxiety about being the only priest in the parish:

> You might be interested in visiting here sometime. It is safer for a visitor than for some of us working here. . . . I know you would enjoy working here. But maybe that can come later, after a few years of experience. My associate still can't be here with me now. It would be nice to have someone here to have Mass and be around for sick calls, etc. Then I could be in and out on an unscheduled basis and feel safer (June 1, 1981).

In concluding his letter to the newly ordained priest, he restated clearly what priesthood meant for him.

> Don, take care of your priesthood. "Service" has to be our motto. I have heard that a certain group of priests in Oklahoma are expecting to be served, rather than to serve. That is one accusation I don't want. . . . Pray for me (*Ibid.*).

Again the same voice, with no pretentious thoughts or high aspirations. His priesthood meant simple, down-to-earth service to his people. For that ideal he lived, and was ready, if necessary, to die.

After Easter Stan was faced with an enormous job. Many young people needed to be prepared for confirmation at Pentecost. The July feast of St. James the Apostle was also approaching, the traditional time for first communions and marriages. Hundreds of people needed instruction and formation. Yet the catechists who had to give the instruction were still paralyzed by the fear of kidnapping. Morale was low and people were slow to cooperate. Stan realized that he had to be firm and direct in order to revitalize the parish after his three-month absence.

There was a general fear of classes . . . because
of the political situation. . . . Finally one
ex-president of Acción [Catholic Action], who
has a pretty good head on him, said that if it
was up to the catechists, nothing would get
done. I just had to order them to do it and it
would get done. Well, I just ordered it to be
done and it is really amazing how it has helped
the catechists themselves and the parish in
general (July 11, 1981).

In a letter to his parents written on July 13th, Stan gave an
idea of the work involved.

We got busy and prepared 149 people for
confirmation on Pentecost Sunday. The sisters
organized the material and I helped teach the
classes to the catechists who in turn had to
teach the groups in the different zones in the
parish. A week after Pentecost we started
classes for the catechists in preparation for the
marriages and first communion for the feast of
St. James the Apostle, the 25th of July. One
of the sisters and I gave classes on marriage to
about eighteen catechists and other sisters
prepared another group of catechists for the
classes for Communion. We have ninety-two
couples to have their marriages blessed and
over 260 will be making their communions. All
this work has done a lot to get the parish in
gear again and to dispel some of the fear of the
past months.

*F*aithful to Death

Stan's energetic activity, strongly inspired by the enthusiasm of his sisters, must have helped him and everyone else to overcome somewhat their fears in the face of increasing violence. But he must have been aware that death was coming closer to him. Before his departure for the United States in January 1981, he wrote much about the killing of Indians; after his return in April his letters more often allude to priests who were the victims of violence. To his friend Frankie he wrote:

Photo of Stan Rother by Frankie Williams.

While I was gone in mid-May [to attend Don's ordination] a priest of the Diocese of Sololá was killed in Tecpan. He had been there just over a year and was a native of Patzún. A month ago a Jesuit was kidnapped on the street in Guatemala City and hasn't been heard from since. [This was Father Louis Edwardo Pellecer, S.J., who later appeared on television to confess his participation in the Revolutionary Army of the Poor (E.G.P.), and to accuse some of his fellow Jesuits of leftist activities. Many who saw him on television are convinced that he was brainwashed and forced to make a false confession. Pellecer has remained in the hands of the military ever since and has not been able to receive any visitors alone.] Ten days ago an Italian Franciscan [Fr. Tulio Maruzzo] was shot in the East, in the Dept. of Isabal. He was with me in Panama almost four years ago for six weeks of update in theology. That makes eight priests killed or kidnapped since May 1, 1980. When does it stop? (July 11, 1981).

In a letter to his friends Mary and Joe, written one day after his letter to Frankie, he asked in his understated way: "Sounds like persecution?" He knew that being a foreigner, even a U.S. citizen, no longer offered him special status. More and more priests had to leave the country to avoid certain death, and Stan did not have any illusions about his own safety. What sustained him were the concrete needs of his people. He thought more about them than about himself.

He visited his parishioner Manuel in the penitentiary, attended to the needs of the widows and orphans, visited the sick and tried to offer help wherever he could. One man especially drew much of his attention. He was kidnapped in February together with others, but to everyone's surprise reappeared during Holy Week with bullet wounds in his legs. Stan found ways to give him the necessary medical attention. Dr. Harsha, a bone specialist from Oklahoma City, went yearly during his vacation to various Third World countries to offer his medical expertise. When he was back in Guatemala, Stan saw a chance to help his wounded parishioner. To his parents he wrote:

> I stopped in Sololá to visit a doctor, a bone specialist, who is there for the month of July. . . . I hope to have him check the guy here who was shot up in February. This guy gets around on crutches and thinks he still has a bullet in the hip (July 13, 1981).

Caring for this man occupied Stan during the last days of his life. His last known act of ministry was to bring his wounded parishioner to Sololá to have the bullet removed and his legs healed.

On July 28, 1981, at about 12:30 a.m. three tall, slender men with masks slipped into the parish rectory. When they failed to find Stan in what they thought was his bedroom, they woke up a young man sleeping in a nearby room. The young man was Francisco Bocel, the brother of Stan's associate, Pedro Bocel. They told Francisco they would kill him if he refused to lead them to Stan. Shaking with fear, Francisco led them downstairs to the room with "walls of rock" where Stan lay sleeping. Francisco called out in Spanish, "Father, they are looking for you."

As Francisco fled upstairs, the men entered the room and tried to kidnap Stan. Realizing immediately what was happening, Stan cried out, "Kill me here!" A grim, unspoken understanding was shared among the priests of the diocese that in the event of a kidnapping attempt it was better to be killed immediately than to be tortured, killed and dumped by the side of the road or in a field. They did not want to cause their people the immense suffering of having to search for their priests' bodies.

The available evidence (skin ripped from his knuckles and blood stains high on the walls of his bedroom) indicates that Stan put up a tough fight against the intruders. Stan didn't cry for help. He knew he had no chance of surviving. His only hope was to die then and there, and avoid being taken. When his kidnappers realized that they couldn't take him alive, they shot him twice in the head and fled, leaving his bleeding body behind.

The shots woke up the sisters who slept in the convent part of the house. Soon after, the sisters found Stan's dead body and realized with a shock what had happened.

The Seed of the Church

Stan died as he lived, fighting for his people. His death was as straightforward, unsentimental, unambiguous and simple as his life. He remained the quiet giant to the very end, not crying out for help but using his physical and moral strength against those who came to harm his people. He didn't fight to stay alive, but battled so he would not end up causing suffering for the people he had served for 13 years. In the end, his faithfulness cost him his life. His letters show that he was prepared. Dietrich Bonhoeffer returned to Germany to fight with his people against the tyranny of Hitler, knowing that it might cost his life. In the same way, Stan Rother returned to Guatemala to be faithful to his own. Stan knew as did Bonhoeffer that he took a great risk, but he didn't want to leave his people alone in their struggle. As he himself said, the worst that could happen to him was to be thought of as having abandoned his people when they needed him most.

He stayed with his people and died for them. He will never be accused of expecting to be served rather than to serve, as one who thought more about himself than about others. He used well the talents he had for the poor who were entrusted to him. In one of his last letters, he mentions that his favorite text is the text of the last judgment in which Christ says: "For I was hungry and you gave me food; I was thirsty and you gave me drink; . . . in so far as you did this to the least of these my brothers and sisters, you did it to me" (Mt 25:35,40). Now, having given his life for the least of Christ's people, he can also expect to hear the conclusion to this text: "Come, you whom my Father has blessed, take for your heritage the kingdom prepared for you since the foundation of the world" (Mt 25:34).

HERE IS MY SERVANT
WHOM I UPHOLD,
MY CHOSEN ONE
IN WHOM MY SOUL DELIGHTS
I HAVE ENDOWED HIM WITH
MY SPIRIT THAT HE MAY
BRING TRUE JUSTICE
TO THE NATIONS.

HE DOES NOT CRY OUT
OR SHOUT ALOUD,
OR MAKE HIS VOICE
HEARD IN THE STREETS
HE DOES NOT BREAK THE CRUSHED REED,
OR QUENCH THE QUIVERING FLAME.
FAITHFULLY HE BRINGS TRUE JUSTICE ;
HE WILL NEVER WAVER, NOR BE CRUSHED,
UNTIL TRUE JUSTICE IS ESTABLISHED
ON EARTH.
—ISAIAH 42:1-4

Father Stanley "Francisco" Rother
BORN MARCH 27, 1935 OKARCHE, OKLAHOMA
MARTYRED JULY 28, 1981
SANTIAGO ATITLAN, GUATEMALA

In all stories of true martyrs, the martyr's death is as much a beginning as an end. Stan's death confirms this. His death was the end of an earthly life of faithful service but the beginning of new life in the hearts of his people, and in all who would learn his story. This became visible in Santiago Atitlán the day after his death. Thousands of people gathered in the church; they brought a vial of Stan's blood and offered it with the blood of Christ at the altar. It became visible in Oklahoma where thousands of people responded in grateful words and grateful action to the news of Stan's gift of himself unto death. It became visible in the decision of the sisters who worked with Stan not to run off in fear, but to stay in the parish and continue the work. It became visible in the life of a young woman named Sylvia, who after hearing the story of Stan's life and death from the sisters, joined their community and dedicated her life to serving the poor. It became visible in many other ways too, but they cannot all be told here.

Except for one! It begins one month after Stan's death. A 38-year-old priest, who had served as a missionary for seven years in Paraguay, was flying to Lima on his way back home. He opened a *Time* magazine on the plane and read that a man he had played basketball and prayed with had been killed in Guatemala. The name of the priest on the plane was John Vesey. A new story had begun.

A New Friendship

I met John Vesey in the summer of 1972 at the Maryknoll language institute in Cochabamba, Bolivia. John had just arrived from his parish in Brooklyn where he worked as an associate pastor, and had come to Cochabamba to prepare himself for his work with Latins in his diocese. Two years later he was appointed to the parish of San Pedro in Coronel Oviedo in Paraguay, a parish adopted by the Brooklyn Diocese. I had just finished my first year on the faculty of Yale Divinity School and wanted to learn more about the church in Latin America. Learning Spanish was essential to both our aspirations. During that summer of 1972 we spent much time together, as we both found ourselves in the same hospital at different periods. First, John became ill with hepatitis, and I visited him. Later, I had to be put in traction because of a pinched nerve in my back, and he visited me!

I soon came to feel a great affection for John. His contagious laugh and vibrant enthusiasm quickly created in me a desire to know him better. He revealed himself to me as a man with a great feel for the gospel, a profound love for people of the most different backgrounds, and an enormous eagerness to learn. He was always surrounded by stacks of letters from his parishioners, and all sorts of books he wanted to read. His vitality was rooted in a life of prayer that united his wide variety of interests and concerns.

I knew from the beginning that he had a lot to teach me even though he kept suggesting that he was my student. John's uninhibited expression of his deep love for Jesus affected me greatly. After years in seminaries and universities I had developed a certain hesitation or even shyness in this respect, but John reconnected me with some of my lost spontaneity. John was far from pious or sentimental, yet he had a nearly childlike directness about his faith that kept disarming me over and over again. When he saw me becoming apprehensive, tense or preoccupied, he usually started to laugh loudly, never giving me much of a chance to become too introspective or melancholic. In the midst of our long conversations he kept suggesting that I was stronger than I thought I was, knew more than I thought I knew, and did better than I thought I did. John is a fine example of someone who is able to grow and mature by loving the people around him so sincerely that they are eager to give him their best. This makes him an excellent priest. He helps people discover how much they are worth, not only in his eyes but in God's eyes.

Father John Vesey speaks with parishioners, members of the Tzutuhíl people.

After our time together in Cochabamba, we stayed in touch, at first by sporadic correspondence and later by visiting each other whenever possible. Since our lives were so different, his in a parish in Paraguay and mine at a university in the United States, there was a long period during which it seemed our friendship would be reduced to a precious memory. But when in 1976 Richard Alan White, a mutual friend, brought us together again in Paraguay, we both realized that our friendship was meant to grow in the service of our common vocation. In Paraguay I realized that John had become an astute observer of the constantly changing political climate in Latin America. Our friend Richard White, one of the most capable analysts of current events in the region, had given John a critical understanding of the realities he encountered. This new and better understanding may have taken away some of his "political innocence," but it certainly led him to a deeper commitment to his pastoral work in the midst of an increasingly violent situation.

John's conviction of the creative and re-creative power of God's word in our world became an increasing source of inspiration for me. Though not a theoretician, he had developed an uncanny sense of what could or could not be trusted, what should or should not be taken seriously, and what was or was not worth following up. His spiritual alertness gave him a rare gift of discernment in the midst of his highly complex and often ambiguous political and socioeconomic context. In the midst of the great variety of opinion about how the church ought to be present in our world, John's spiritually based judgments offered me much hope, courage, and confidence.

A salient aspect of John's spirituality is his great love for
the saints. It was always important for him to stay in close
touch with the great saints who have played a central role
in the growth and development of the Christian faith. He
considers them members of his family who deserve regular
attention and even visits. Thus, when his bishop, Francis J.
Mugavero, called him back from Paraguay to Brooklyn in
1981, John didn't return before having prayed in Lima at the
graves of the great saints of Latin America: Rose of Lima,
Martin de Porres and Juan Massias. He felt a need to
connect his life with theirs and thus to discern what his new
relationship would be with the Latin American people he had
served for nearly a decade. It was during this pilgrimage that
Stan Rother entered his life again. As soon as he read about
Stan's martyrdom, he knew that Stan would have something
to do with the way his life would develop. Although it would
take three years for him to learn the full implications of Stan's
death, Stan never left his heart and mind again. The casual
friend of the seminary, who had hardly crossed his mind for
many years, had re-entered his life with new force and was
now there to stay. Talking about Stan's reappearance in his
life, John says:

> When I picked up that old issue of *Time* on the
> plane and read that Stan was dead, the first
> thought that came to me was: "Here I am,
> healthy, safe, and going home, and Stan is
> dead." For the first time I understood what
> survivor's guilt was. I thought: "Why am I alive,
> why me?" It was incredibly painful. In Lima I
> said Mass for Stan and his family at the altar of
> Rose of Lima, Martin de Porres and Juan
> Massias and prayed: "Lord, if you want me to
> take Stan's place, I am willing!

Upon leaving Lima, John was invited to attend a meeting about family planning in Bogota, Colombia, orgainized by the Conference of Latin American Bishops. There he met Sister Frances Kearns, who worked in Guatemala. She told John much more about Stan and his ministry. John learned of the remarkable effect of Stan's life and death upon the people of Santiago Atitlán. He heard as well of their firm belief that Stan continued to intercede for them in heaven and concern himself with their welfare. Thus, John developed a sense of solidarity with the people of Santiago Atitlán and their departed priest.

Sentir con la Iglesia:
To Feel With the Church

When John came back to Brooklyn, a process of
discernment began. He slowly had to come to know where
God was calling him next. His first concern was his own
health. In contrast to Stan, John struggles with his health.
Not only was he plagued with hepatitis, but he also suffered
from recurring kidney stones. While in this respect he was an
unlikely candidate for the life of a missionary, his strong
conviction and iron will compensated amply for his poor
health. Besides caring for his health, John studied theology at
St. John's University and made a 30-day retreat in Syracuse,
New York. At this time, John also became involved in the
aftermath of the assassination of the four U.S. churchwomen
in El Salvador.

In December 1980, eight months after Archbishop
Romero had been assassinated in El Salvador, Ita Ford,
Maura Clarke, Jean Donovan and Dorthy Kazel were
kidnapped by Salvadoran security forces near the airport.
After the soldiers raped, tortured and executed them, their
broken bodies were dumped into a shallow sandy grave. Ita
was raised in Brooklyn, Maura in Queens; both were
Maryknoll Sisters from John's Diocese of Brooklyn, New
York. The more John learned about the lives and ministry of
these women the harder he worked not only to keep their
memory alive but also to see to it that the true nature of their
martyrdom would become known and celebrated by the
church. Whenever John speaks of the four women a special
energy bursts forth from him:

U.S. churchwomen slain in El Salvador in 1980: Clockwise from top left are Sister Ita
Ford, Sister Maura Clarke, Sister Dorothy Kazel, and Jean Donovan.

Missionaries were being killed, two of them
from my own diocese. I am a missionary. I
have always been taught about the communion
of saints, the unity among Christians living and
dead. How could we possibly forget these
women who had given their lives for doing
what we, the church, had sent them out to do?
Is their death not a call for us to continue their
work? They were murdered for their faith! They
took the gospel seriously. They helped the
poor, brought food to the hungry, medicine to
the sick. They cared for displaced persons and
refugees. It often seems that we in the U.S.
church are ashamed of them, and run away
from them as if they are an embarrassment for
us. There should be strong solidarity among us
Christians and especially among missionaries.
We must honor our martyrs and lift them up as
signs of hope for the church, because they are
reminders of God's loving presence.

John had found a new mission in his work for these North
American martyrs. He shows a holy indignation when
mentioning the testimonies of former Secretary of State
Alexander Haig and of U.S. Ambassador to the United
Nations, Jeane Kirkpatrick, who both spoke about the
women as subversives. In John's words:

> Many church people began to have doubts
> about their obvious martyrdom, because official
> representatives of the U.S. government
> attacked them after their deaths, slandered and
> slurred them. This is what happened to martyrs
> in the early church. Their enemies tried to
> destroy their reputations and villify their names.
> Many in the church identify closely with the
> U.S. Government, which justifies most of its
> foreign policy by advertising it as a heroic battle
> against communism. They are more inclined to
> believe the Catholics in the State Department,
> who called the churchwomen "naive" and
> "political activists," than the blood witness of
> their own faithful martyrs.

The more John studied the life and martyrdom of the four women, the more he was convinced of the importance of making their true story known. He urgently claimed them as contemporary saints who could strengthen the faith of the Christian community, in whose name they had lived and died. He urged the sister senate of his diocese and later his priest senate and many religious communities to go to work, saying:

Let us ask Congress for an official investigation
into the churchwomen's deaths, so that the
truth may be revealed and set us free from our
petty ideological bickering. Let us fight the
calumny and look closely at their lives and
deaths, so that we will recognize their
wholehearted commitment to the gospel and
confess our own sinfulness in not giving them
the place in our church they deserve. Why
are we afraid to look at the martyrdom of these
women whom we sent to the missions in the
name of Christ? How is God going to bless us
if we are not faithful to the witness of our own
martyrs? How are we going to inspire young
people when we hesitate to lift up these women
as exemplars of faith and courage? Who wants
to be a member of a cowardly church, a
faithless community?

While in Brooklyn, John helped mount a petition drive
to persuade Congress to investigate thoroughly the deaths of
the women. For him this work was not simply political. He
saw it as a way to make U.S. Christians aware of how their
brother and sister Christians were witnessing to the poor and
embattled Christ of El Salvador. He felt that petitioning for an
investigation was the best way to awaken a sense of
responsibility among U.S. Christians for their sisters and
brothers in Central America. John wanted to make real the
motto of Archbishop Romero, *Sentir con la Iglesia*, "To Feel
with the Church," especially the church of the poor and the
oppressed.

During this year in the United States, John became concerned that many Christians had substituted all sorts of issues for the gospel: peace issues, third world issues, women's issues, nuclear issues. He saw much debate, many arguments and political demonstrations, but missed the awareness of being the people of God, a community of Jesus' disciples. He missed the sense that we are a people not bound by national boundaries but able to embrace all believers, and all people wherever they might be, with the love of the living Christ. The women who gave their lives in El Salvador didn't die for a cause or an issue but for their people, in whom they had recognized the face of their suffering Lord. Archbishop Romero had not asked them to solve political or economic problems, but simply to work with the refugees in El Salvador. He wanted his displaced people to know and see that Christians from other countries came to be with them, pray with them and help them obtain food, shelter and medical care. The women gave their lives for these people. John hoped that their deaths would bear fruit in the lives of the many North Americans who would hear their story.

During his first months home John didn't forget Stan Rother, yet he made no immediate request to be sent to Guatemala. He first wanted simply to go and see the place where Stan had lived and died. In July 1982, John flew to Mexico City and Cuernavaca to study in more detail the situation in Central America. Richard Alan White, our mutual friend, had by this time become a noted Latin American scholar, and was based in Cuernavaca. Richard served as John's host and supervisor during this period. From Mexico he went to El Salvador to pray at the graves of Ita and Maura. From there, he journeyed to Santiago Atitlán, in Guatemala. During this first visit to Santiago John was overwhelmed by the living memory of Stan. The sisters who continued his work spoke of him as their father, and without hesitation called him a saint. The leaders of the town said, "He was a martyr," and the bishop who came to confer the sacrament of confirmation declared as well, "He was killed for his faith." John soon realized that the people were eagerly waiting for someone from Oklahoma to take Stan's place. They were praying fervently for Stan's successor.

From Visitation Parish to Santiago Atitlán

In November 1982, Bishop Mugavero appointed John to be associate pastor of Visitation Parish in the Redhook section of Brooklyn. He would stay there until July 1984. When I visited John at Visitation Parish, he took my friend Jeff Merkel and me on a walk through the streets of the Redhook district. It soon became clear to me why wearing a Roman collar is not such a bad idea after all. It certainly makes you feel a little safer! We conversed with members of a motorcycle gang, talked with several Hispanic teenagers, and walked through "The Projects"—a housing complex with a dangerous reputation. Finally we crossed a little park, a favorite place for drug trafficking. Reflecting recently on his time there John said:

> I wouldn't have missed it for anything in the world. It was a rough but very challenging time for me. I certainly didn't have to go to Latin America to see real problems. "Visitation" was full of them. But good, very good people. Sixty-five percent black and 20 percent Hispanic. Fifty percent of the people lived under the poverty line. Many needs, much agony, much work for a priest. It was hard, it was true missionary work, and it made me grow. I loved it!

Although John was happy at Visitation Parish and grateful for what he learned there, he knew in his heart that he would have to return south. His years in Paraguay had created a hunger and thirst that could not be fully satisfied in Brooklyn. Meanwhile, his work on behalf of the martyrs of El Salvador increased. He developed a close relationship with Ita Ford's mother and her brother Bill. He mobilized people for his petition drive by giving many talks together with Mrs. Ford, and publishing a series of articles in the diocesan paper about the church in Central America. During this period his desire to take Stan Rother's place in Santiago became stronger and deeper. What had started as a vague wish had grown into a trustworthy desire.

He finally wrote to Archbishop Charles Salatka of Oklahoma City, asking to be considered as a possible successor to Stan. Archbishop Salatka wrote back that he and Bishop Melotto considered it too dangerous to send another priest to Santiago at that time. John was not disappointed with this response. He told me that the right time would come and that he would just have to wait for it. He was convinced that going to Central America without a clear sense of being sent by the church was foolish. He would never go simply because there was work to do and he wanted to do it. He would go only if he had the full approval, support and sympathy of the hierarchy. He knew that his ministry could never be fruitful unless he was truly "sent" and had the full blessing of the community to which he belonged and its leaders. He saw the martyrdom of Oscar Romero, the U.S. churchwomen and Stan Rother as rooted in their obedience to the church. Wanting to walk in their footsteps, he could not imagine himself doing anything that was not truly ecclesial; however much he needed to go, he knew he had to be sent.

In February 1984, John wrote again to Archbishop
Salatka. For a long time he didn't hear anything. Around
Easter, the Archbishop called and invited him to Oklahoma
to discuss his possible appointment to Santiago Atitlán. After
this meeting, events rushed by in rapid succession. In May,
John flew to Oklahoma and was interviewed by the
personnel board of the archdiocese. Talking about that
experience he says:

> They asked me many penetrating questions, but
> the most difficult was: "How do you feel about
> taking the place of a martyr?" It was that
> question that started to make me hesitant. Was
> I really ready to go? Wasn't I too self-assured?
> Maybe I wasn't the right person to take Stan's
> place. I became so doubtful that I asked them
> for some time to pray over my decision.

But John's hesitation didn't last long. After a few days at home, he wrote Archbishop Salatka that he was ready to go. On June 5th, during a Tulsa-Oklahoma City clergy week, John addressed the priests. He spoke mainly about Stan, and suggested that the priests of Oklahoma claim Stan as their saint and work for his canonization. "We diocesan priests have lost our historical sense," he said. "If Stan had been a Jesuit, 20 books would have been written about him by now. Let us remember him and be proud that one of our brothers has given his life for his people, following the example of our Lord Jesus."

After speaking before the priests, all John's earlier doubts were gone. Now he knew that working in Paraguay, reading about Stan's death on his way home, working for the slain churchwomen, and ministering to the poor in the Redhook district were not a series of disconnected events, but ways in which God had been preparing him for his new mission.

Yet there still remained a gnawing question within. Stan was a martyr and John was placing himself in the same dangerous position. Challenged by concerned friends, family and colleagues who feared for his life, John spent hours praying, trying to fathom the depth of his convictions. Placing yourself in a situation in which you are almost sure to be killed is an indirect form of suicide. Was it possible that he was courting danger because of some kind of unconscious death wish or martyr-complex?

In the end, the answer behind these troubling questions was quite simple. John Vesey clearly saw that his call to Guatemala was based on his profound connection with Stan Rother, and in his obedience to the most basic teachings of Christianity.

The mission ceremony in which John was officially sent to Santiago Atitlán gave him a great feeling of joy and peace merged with a sense of the seriousness of his call. He was grateful for all that had led him to that moment, and longed to go at last to the Tzutuhíl Indians, who since July 28, 1981, had been praying that a priest would be sent to continue Padre A'plas' work.

On July 25th, the feast of St. James, John started his new task in Santiago Atitlán—almost three years to the day after Stan's death.

Father Vesey enjoys a moment with some children.

A Call to Prayer

From the moment John told me he was going to
Guatemala to take Stan's place, I knew I had to be with him
in the early stages of his ministry. Our friendship had
developed over the years; while John may once have viewed
me more as a giver than a receiver, by the time he left for
Santiago I had come to think of him as a mentor who kept
my eyes fixed on Jesus and challenged me on the hard road
of faithfulness. Friendship has always belonged to the core of
my spiritual journey. God has given me many friends, and
each of them has played a significant role in my thinking,
feeling, speaking and acting. Some of these friendships have
been intense, painful and marked by turmoil, while others
have been calm, steady and gentle. Since 1972, John has
been a good friend even though we did not see much of
each other. But as I came to know his vision, I began to
realize that my friendship with John was emerging as an
important part of my own vocation as a priest. I started to
share with him more of my own joy and sorrow and let him
see my struggles. I became aware that John had been given
to me as a waiting presence, a friend who would be there at
crucial moments. John had strongly encouraged me to go to
Latin America. But when I eventually realized that Latin
America—at least for the near future—would not be my
permanent home, he helped me see the positive and hope-
giving implications of that realization. In some way, John's
ongoing search for God's will and my own had become
intertwined. When he decided to go to Guatemala, I knew
his decision would affect my life in some way.

During his years in Brooklyn, John often referred to the
central place of prayer in the Christian life. What might have
sounded sentimental or escapist when spoken by someone
who had not done or seen so much, became an authoritative
message when proclaimed after long years of involvement in
the struggle of the poor of Latin America. When John spoke
of prayer, he knew what he was talking about. The opposite
of an escape from the bitter realities of an oppressed people,
prayer is the way to both the heart of God and the heart of
the world—precisely because they have been joined through
the suffering of Jesus Christ. He knew that those who pray
cry out with the suffering Christ to the God who has created
the world out of love and yearns to see the world return to
that love. He knew that those who are poor, homeless,
hungry and in agony are not just individuals hopelessly
scattered over the face of the earth, but men, women and
children intimately loved by a Father who works for their
liberation and waits with tears in his eyes for them to come
home. He knew that praying is letting one's own heart
become the place where the tears of God and the tears of
God's children can merge and become tears of hope.

These are not John's words; they are my own. I cannot
use other words to speak about prayer. Yet John's friendship
and the way God shaped his life inspire me to write them. I
had to go to Santiago Atitlán to pray with John and his
people. I had gone to many places to learn a language, get
to know people, admire art and become familiar with another
culture, but I had never gone very far just to pray. But that is
what John invited me to do—"Come here to pray," he said
when we spoke on the telephone—and I knew that this was
the only reason to go.

When Peter and I arrived in Santiago we began to understand the full meaning of John's invitation. John is anything but someone who sits quietly in a corner with his eyes closed and his hands folded in his lap. He has nothing of the monk about him. He is moving, talking, calling, planning, organizing, teaching and preaching all the time. He jokes, laughs and teases whenever he has a chance. He hides little and shows his heart to anyone who wants to see it. Yet all of this belongs to his prayer. Prayer is living in unceasing communion with God and God's people and thus seeing and proclaiming the rightful order of things, the divine order. Prayer is living in the heart of God—a heart of justice, peace and righteous.

Prayer requires teaching, so that we never forget the God who wants to bind our hearts to his. Prayer requires preaching, so that our hearts do not grow cold and turn away from God who desires our love. Prayer requires baptism, confession, the eucharist, confirmation, marriage and the sacrament of the sick, so that at every point in our lives we can reunite ourselves with the God who offers us his own house to live in. Prayer requires celebration to remind us that God calls us together to acknowledge his love in acts of supplication, gratitude and praise. Prayer also requires sowing and reaping, weaving and sculpting, buying and selling, digging and building, and all other forms of human labor so that the beauty of God's creation can be revealed through the work of our hands. All indeed is prayer. But only through a deeply committed ministry can this statement become true for us—we who are constantly tempted to let ourselves be disconnected from the source of our lives.

All of this became most visible during the Sunday afternoon Eucharist in the church of Santiago. John stood behind the altar in a white alb and a brilliant colored stole made by the people of the town. Before him more than 2,000 women, men and children, dressed in the rich colors of the Tzutuhíl people, had gathered to pray. As soon as John began the Eucharistic Prayer, the people started to pour out their prayers in loud voices. Everyone expressed their own fears and hopes, asked their own favors, gave their own thanks, and sang their own praise. The church was filled with a crescendo of thousands of cries, raised in supplication and praise. As I experienced this symphony of prayer, I felt all things human being gathered together around the body and blood of Christ and made into one great Eucharistic Prayer.

All the people became priests and lifted up their lives together with the bread and the wine. The people became one body, the body of Christ, dying on the cross and rising again in glory. Misery and delight, despair and hope, fear and love, death and life—all became one in this wave of prayer that finally flowed into the prayer that Jesus himself taught us, the Our Father.

"I want you to come to pray with me and my people," John had said. Now I saw what he meant, and recognized better than ever before that we must make our lives into one unceasing prayer.

*P*rayer and Martyrdom

John's call to prayer, however, has a much deeper meaning when we see it in the context of the reality in which he has chosen to live. Violence in Guatemala continues to be part of the daily experience of the people. More and more names are added to the list of the disappeared. Alvaro René Sosa Ramos, a former trade union leader kidnapped by Guatemalan government security forces on March 11, 1984, is one of the few who has escaped to tell the story of what goes on in the torture chambers of Guatemala.

> With handcuffs on they forced me to strip.
> They tied up my feet and hung me head down.
> Afterwards I was beaten with a hatchet handle
> while they accused me of belonging to a
> Guatemalan revolutionary organization
> . . . . They took turns beating me. When they
> came in smoking, they would put out their
> cigarettes on my body. They would leave me
> alone for a few minutes and then the next one
> would come in.

I remember that one "Kaibil" [member of the Guatemalan Army's elite counterinsurgency troops] hit me in the face with his belt buckle. Since it was a huge belt buckle, he broke my eyebrow with one of the blows. When they weren't hitting me, I could hear the blows and screams of other kidnap victims. I lost all sense of how long I was there being tortured. They took me down from where I hung and threw me on the floor.

A few hours later they hung me by the feet again and a "Kaibil" came in especially to kick me in the face. After suffering those kicks, I was taken down to go and see another man who was hung in the same way.

They asked me if I knew him. He was deformed by the tortures but I could recognize Silvio Matricardi Salam whom I had known when he was President of the National Teachers' Organization and I was the trade union leader at the Diana products factory.

I was very moved to see his body so deformed because of the blows and I immediately told them that I did not know that man. When they returned they hung me up again. This time they began to apply electric shocks to my body.

It is incredible how violently the body jumps up and strikes against the wall. Sometimes I tried to have my head hit in such a way that I might lose consciousness, but I couldn't. After the electric shocks the body remains burning with heat. I was thirsty and asked for water.

During the torture I heard water running, but they didn't give me any. (Information Bulletin of Guatemala Human Rights Commission/U.S.A. June 1984, pp. 5-6).

This description gives us some idea of the immense suffering of thousands of Guatemalan people. Some of them were Stan's catechists. Since the Kaibiles want to keep their operation completely hidden, they do not allow anyone to survive. After extorting from their victims whatever knowledge they may have about others, they kill them and often throw their mutilated bodies by the side of the road to terrorize the people even more. Most bodies, however, are never seen again, adding to the growing number of people who simply disappear.

With a proper burial, a death, even a murder, can be mourned and life can go on. But the uncertainty of a disappeared person's fate adds a new dimension to human suffering. The families never know for sure the fate of their loved ones and many simply refuse to give up hope that somehow they are still alive. This agony is so widespread that recently groups have formed throughout Latin America in the hope of finding some answers about these missing people. There is even a hemisphere-wide coalition of these groups, the Latin American Federation of Family Associations of the Detained-Disappeared. According to this human rights organization, more than 90,000 people in Latin America have disappeared because of their political beliefs in recent years.

When Pope John Paul II visited Guatemala in March 1983 he said:

> Faith teaches us that humanity is the image and likeness of God . . . and that when people are abused . . . when flagrant injustices are committed against them, when they are tortured, kidnapped, or their right to life violated, a crime and most serious offense are committed against the Creator (John Paul II, Campo de Marte homily, 5; English translation from *LADOC*, Nov./Dec. 1984, p. 10).

On June 10, 1984, the Guatemalan Bishops' Conference issued a pastoral letter in which they added their own words to those of John Paul:

> We, the bishops of Guatemala, want to make very clear our mission in the promotion, defense and guarding of human rights. . . . In the present historical moment, the Church has the right and the obligation . . . to denounce, in a manner consistent with the gospel, the injustices and situations of sin which attack human dignity and trample on human rights, and to call those responsible to reflect and repent. The Church will have to carry out the mission of announcing and denouncing because it wants to be faithful to the mission which its Divine Founder conferred upon it, even when it means being misunderstood, slandered, and persecuted (English translation published in *LADOC*, Nov./Dec. 1984, p. 10).

When John Vesey converted the bedroom where Stan was murdered into a chapel, he acted in the spirit of John Paul II and the Guatemalan bishops. Acting against our instinctual human tendency to avoid places touched by death as frightening or "spooky," John made Stan's room a place of prayer in which the cry for justice could be heard. Instead of asking people to forget the tragic events of the past and go on with their lives as if nothing had happened, he urged them to remember Stan's death, and draw strength from his memory in their daily struggle for dignity. Instead of maintaining a prudent and safe silence about the man who had given his life for the defense of his people, John didn't let a blessing, teaching or sermon pass without loudly declaring Stan's courage and faith. Stan's martyrdom was constantly lifted up to resist the power of death and proclaim faith in the victory of the Lord of Life. Every time the pastor and people of Santiago pray, they pray with a faith strengthened by their martyr's blood.

A lay catechist distributes communion in Santiago Atitlán.

When Peter and I saw John surrounded by thousands of loudly praying Tzutuhíl Indians, we saw clearly how much hope their new priest was giving them. They had asked God for a pastor to continue their Father's work. They had prayed for three years, and now he had come. Indeed, the light is stronger than the darkness, love is stronger than fear, and life is stronger than death. No one can say that John is safer than Stan, but everyone knows that Stan's death has not been in vain, and that John's is a life they want to celebrate as long as they can.

Wearing a Tzutuhíl stole, Vesey preaches a homily.

One morning a group of women came to the rectory and offered John a beautiful red, yellow and gold shawl they had woven for him. It was the same type of shawl that Stan had received as a sign of honor after many years of service. But the women of Santiago Atitlán wanted their new priest, Padre Juan, to wear that same sign now, even though he had just arrived. Thus he would be fully aware of the prayers, support and love of his people. When they gave him this symbol of their trust and confidence, John knew better than a few months earlier the answer to the question: "How do you feel about taking the place of a martyr?" He felt a strong call to pray with his people, and be faithful in the struggle to overcome violence and discover a new freedom to love.

Prayer and martyrdom are intimately connected. When the early Christians were no longer required to become martyrs, that is, witnesses for the Lord with their blood, many became "confessors," witnesses through a life of unceasing prayer. If ever I saw the connection between martyrdom and prayer, it was in Guatemala. When malnutrition, poor health, poor housing, low pay, and long, tiring work mark life every day; when terror fills the air and torture and death are a constant threat, the human heart has to choose between despair and hope, between resignation to the power of darkness or a defiant reaching out to the light, between victimization and liberation. It is an inner choice, not dependent on outer conditions but on the will to claim one's freedom whatever the circumstances. To cry out to the God of life in the midst of darkness, to hold on to joy while walking in a valley of tears, to keep speaking of peace when sounds of war fill the air—that is what prayer is about. It is indeed a clinging to the Lord when all is being torn apart by greed, hatred, violence and war. It is the heartfelt knowledge that

Nothing . . . can come between us and the love
of Christ, even if we are troubled or worried, or
being persecuted, or lacking food or clothes, or
being threatened, or even attacked. As scripture
promised: "for your sake we are being
massacred daily, and reckoned as sheep for the
slaughter." These are the trials through which
we triumph, by the power of him who loved us
(Rom 8: 35-37).

In its pure form, prayer is the divine breath of those
whom the world tries to suffocate with terror. Prayer is the
martyrdom of those who live.

*P*roclaiming the Message, Welcome or Unwelcome

John was not in Santiago very long before he was called to experience this truth personally. A disturbing series of events occurred. On one of the first nights in his new parish, John heard a drunken man sing outside his window, "First we killed Padre Francisco. Next we will kill Padre Juan." It was a drunken man's song but could not be dismissed as just a prank. John spoke of it with a smile that couldn't dispel all his fear. A few weeks later, a man from San Lucas told him that the government had ordered a more detailed "study" of the situation in Santiago Atitlán. And when Peter, John and I arrived in Guatemala City, church officials told us of rumors that the government was keeping a special eye on Santiago Atitlán. We learned that the military might be preparing to "relocate" parts of its population.

As drunken songs, insinuations, rumors and vague predictions start merging it becomes very hard not to become paralyzed by fear. But John, who knows who, where and why he is, seems quite able to keep fear at a healthy distance, and let his love for his people motivate him in his daily life. John is a happy man. He is deeply grateful for his new task, knows he is called to be in Santiago, feels supported by the church, and loved by the sisters, the people, and his many friends at home. He keeps his heart deeply rooted in the love of Jesus. There is an obvious foolishness in going to a place where your life is in constant danger. As I ponder my life at the university and his life among the Tzutuhíl Indians, I imagine John using the ironic words of Paul to the Corinthians:

> It seems to me, God has put us apostles at the
> end of his parade, with the people sentenced to
> death; it is true—we have been put on show in
> front of the whole universe, angels as well as
> humans. Here we are, fools for the sake of
> Christ, while you are the learned ones in Christ;
> we have no power, but you are influential; you
> are celebrities, we are nobodies (1 Cor 4:9-11).

Every time John spoke to his people during the time
Peter and I stayed with him, I was struck by his lack of fear.
He used plain words that needed no interpretation. They
were the words of the teachers and prophets of Israel, the
apostles and evangelists, and of Jesus himself. They were
words I had heard often before in Holland, France and the
United States. But in Guatemala they were like the double-
edged sword coming from the mouth of the Son of Man (see
Revelation 1:16, 2:12). Words about justice and peace,
forgiveness and reconciliation, conversion and new ways of
living together that had never shocked me before, now struck
me as extremely dangerous. Stan used them and he was
killed; John is using them and he risks his life. They are not
used to irritate or provoke, but to proclaim the truth of God's
kingdom.

In Guatemala one does not have to invent new words or
concepts to be considered a threat. Even the words of Mary,
the mother of Jesus, can be considered subversive.

> My soul proclaims the greatness of the Lord
>   and my spirit exults in God my savior; . . .
> He has shown the power of his arm,
> he has routed the proud of heart.
> He has pulled down princes from their thrones
>   and exalted the lowly.
> The hungry he has filled with good things,
>   the rich he has sent empty away (Lk
>   1:46-47, 51-53).

In Santiago Atitlán, such words can make someone run to the military and denounce you as a communist trying to incite revolution. But John never points an accusing finger at anyone. He invites people to conversion, to a reshaping of heart and mind in the service of Jesus. In one of his homilies he said:

> Nobody is killed by a gun without first being killed by the tongue. We need a new heart, because only from a new heart can peace be born.

"De un corazon nuevo nace la paz," from a new heart peace is born. These words, first used by John Paul II in his 1984 World Day of Peace message, were heard many times by the people of Santiago who came to listen to their new shepherd. These words sound sweet and beautiful. Yet when spoken to people, some of whom have pointed their finger at others who were subsequently kidnapped, tortured and killed, they become something quite different. In the mouth of the shepherd the sweet words of peace become a courageous and radical call to conversion, which may not always be received with gratitude. I saw in practice Paul's admonition to Timothy:

> Before God and before Christ Jesus who is to be judge of the living and the dead, I put this duty to you, in the name of his Appearing and of his kingdom: proclaim the message and, welcome or unwelcome, insist on it. Refute falsehood, correct error, call to obedience—but do all with patience and with the intention of teaching. . . . Be careful always to choose the right course; be brave under trials; make the preaching of the Good News your life's work, in thoroughgoing service (2 Tm 4:1-5).

John is sent, sent as a missionary. He has gone to Guatemala not to buy land, start a business, find cheap labor, or become wealthy. No, he came in service of the Word. This Word came to him not as a possession but as a gift which he announces in season and out of season. The Word is greater than the messenger. Messengers come and go, but the Word remains. This commitment to a Word greater than himself explains John's joy and peace in the midst of danger. It is the joy and peace of the apostles and all who follow in their footsteps.

When family and friends of John called Peter and me after our return from Guatemala and asked: "Is John safe?", we had to simply say: "No, he is not safe but he is very, very happy. Pray for him, don't worry and trust that Stan protects him. He is doing God's work." For those who believe in the coming of the kingdom these are words of consolation. For those who don't they are probably pure nonsense, but there are no other words to express his situation.

In fact, though, John is a busy man who seldom has time to think about his own safety. What keeps him going so fearlessly are his people, of whom the Guatemalan bishops say, "Only God knows the infinite suffering that our people have had to undergo, especially the most humble and defenseless. . . " (*LADOC*, Nov./Dec. 1984, p. 6). It is these people John loves and won't leave. Just like Stan.

*H*ome and Beyond

On Tuesday, September 4th, John brought Peter and me back to Guatemala City. Late that evening the three of us celebrated the Eucharist together in a small, private chapel. It was an intimate time filled with gratitude for the past and hope for the future. This hope was certainly not built on optimism about the political or economical future of Guatemala. At present, Guatemala gives little reason to be optimistic. Our hope is built on the truth that we had gathered in the Name of Jesus and that he indeed is in our midst. While the three of us stood around the table, listened to God's word and broke bread together, I realized that no distance would be able to separate us again. When it is the Lord himself who binds us together, the table from which he feeds us becomes as wide as the whole world. Boston and Santiago Atitlán are no longer two distant cities, but simply two places around God's table. The Eucharist clarified for us the nature of true friendship. Peter, John and I are united by much more than common concerns, histories and sensitivities. We share in a divine affection that became tangible in the bread and cup we offered to each other. "This is the body of Christ, broken for you. This is the blood of Christ, shed for you." How could we not be united when the bond of our friendship is rooted in words like these?

I felt grateful to Peter for having come with me and having become part of my friendship with John. Peter and I could now encourage one another to be faithful to the Lord who had brought the three of us together. I felt grateful to John for showing me concretely the way the Lord had guided him, and for showing me more clearly the ways the Lord was making himself known to me as well. I felt grateful to Stan, whose martyrdom had so forcefully emerged as the light showing us the living presence of God among his people.

When Peter and I left the next morning, John kept waving until he lost sight of us moving through the various checkpoints at the airport. I realized how much our visit had meant to him, and indeed, to all of us. An old friendship was deepened, a new friendship made, a ministry affirmed, a vocation strengthened, and a new way to work together had become manifest. As the plane left the ground and the clouds gradually shrouded the beautiful Guatemalan countryside, we looked at each other and spontaneously said "Thank you." To the God who sent us and brought us together we also said "Thank you." We had traveled between two worlds and found them one. Something new was building, strong and beautiful, marvelous in our eyes. *"De un corazon nuevo nace la paz"*: from a new heart peace is born.

Epilogue

Nearly six months have passed since I wrote the last words of our story. When Peter and I left Guatemala we did not realize that the same dark powers which surrounded and finally took the life of Stan Rother would also close in on John. The drunken man's song proved to be the song of others as well. As John persisted in speaking the word of him who was destined for the fall and rising of many, old resentments, jealousies, angers, suspicions and even hatreds started to re-emerge. The few in Santiago Atitlán who had been glad to see Stan "vanish" soon looked at John with similar eyes. They were willing to enter into deadly coalition with their own oppressors—civilian and military appointees in the village—and were soon able to create an atmosphere that made Santiago unsafe for John.

Within a few months, the sisters felt it was no longer prudent for John to walk around town alone. So one of the sisters began to accompany him wherever he went. Soon it became clear that a more drastic solution was needed. John's friends advised him to leave town and remain in hiding until tension eased. Meanwhile, the bishops of Oklahoma sent Father Thomas McSherry to Santiago to join him in the pastoral work. As the days wore on, many people started to worry about John: bishops in Guatemala and Oklahoma, the sisters with whom he worked and his priest friends in the area, his parishioners in Santiago and his family in New York, even the U.S. Embassy and State Department. Often the remark was made: "We do not want another martyr."

Although this remark was uttered by many, the motives of each who spoke it were quite different. Thus, John became caught in a network of concerned people, a network so ambiguous, confusing and complicated that remaining in Santiago became less and less likely.

After Christmas, John left the parish in the hands of Father McSherry and the sisters and returned to the U.S. He went home in order to visit his family, consult with his bishops, and find some inner and outer space to reflect on the direction in which God was calling him. John burns with desire to return to Santiago and serve the Indian people, whom he came to love so much during the short time he had lived with them. When Stan returned, he lost his life. John is willing to give *his* life, but above all he wants to follow God's way. It might prove a different way than the one Stan had traveled. He is now waiting patiently—and oh how impatiently! He knows that the poor of Guatemala are waiting too: for God, for freedom, and maybe for him.

As this story went to press, we learned that the bishop of Sololá had called John back to Guatemala. On April 10, 1985, John was installed as pastor of San Pedro la Laguna, another Indian town near Lake Atitlán. As we continue to stay in touch, we share both his joy and his fear. We pray that Jesus, the Lord of life, will keep us rooted in a love which overcomes death and casts out all fear.

Father Henri Nouwen is among the foremost of contemporary spiritual writers. A priest from the Netherlands he has been in the United States for many years, teaching at Notre Dame, Yale and Harvard Universities. He is the author of 18 books, among them the continual bestsellers *With Open Hands* and *Out of Solitude* (Ave Maria Press). Other well-known books include *The Wounded Healer, Reaching Out, Genesee Diary* (Doubleday), and *Gracias* (Harper and Row).